Introductio

It's no secret that *Fifty Shades of Grey,* the book by E.L. James which was turned into a movie, has become a national phenomenon. As a result, it sparked a huge interest in the previously taboo world of Bondage, Domination, Sadism, and Masochism (BDSM). For those of you who don't know, *Fifty Shades* is the story of a rich and powerful man named Christian Grey, who seduces a naïve young woman named Anastasia, and entices her to participate in his kinky fantasies of sex slave role playing games.

Until *Fifty Shades* captivated the nation and titillated our imaginations, BDSM games were considered to be sick, twisted, and morally reprehensible, but the books popularity amongst regular everyday people created a newfound interest in the culture and a curiosity for how the games are played. Now, regular men and women just like yourself are asking themselves, *Would I enjoy playing kinky sex games with my partner, and would it make our sexual relationship even better?* The only way to find out is with a little experimentation. In the following pages I will walk you through some fun, safe, and easy ways to try and heat up the fire in your bedroom *Fifty Shades* style and you can determine for yourself if you could be the next Christian Grey or Anastasia Steele.

What is Domination and Submission?

In the story *Fifty Shades of Grey*, Christian Grey introduces Anastasia Steele to the world of BDSM by asking her to play the role of the Submissive or "Slave" in partnership with his role as the Dominant or "Master". These games are not for everyone, but if you have a willing partner, they can be extremely exciting and sensual.

Dominants and Submissives

In BDSM games the Dominant, or Dom for short, is the person in charge within the realm of the game. The Dom is responsible for the safety and well being of their Submissive. Male dominants are often called Sir or Master and female dominants are often called Mistress. However, some Doms like to use nicknames or various tittles for fun. To be a Dominant, you must enjoy being in control and have the capacity and desire to ensure the safety of your play partner. It is not a free pass to simply boss someone else around and requires a great deal of responsibility.

The Submissive, Sub, or "Slave" in the relationship is the person who must obey all commands made by the Dominant.   For many people, this sounds demeaning, but for individuals who want to be freed from having to make any decisions, this can be very soothing and allows them to relax so they can simply enjoy sexual pleasure. To be a Submissive, you must be willing to surrender all your decisions and choices to someone you trust and obey that person in all things, knowing that they will take care of you.

Despite what many people think, the Submissive actually holds all the power in these games. The Dominant must have the Submissives full consent at all times and must stop the game immediately the moment the Submissive wants them to. For the game to be successful both partners will enjoy erotic and sensual pleasure as the Dominant controls the Submissive and the two willingly perform sexual acts upon each other in role playing scenarios they both agree to. The results can be deliciously satisfying for both partners and elevates them to new heights of intimacy and pleasure.

Contracts

People who are experienced in playing Domination/Submissive sex games and want to commit to their relationships sometimes sign contracts with each other or participate in "Collaring" ceremonies. These acts are purely symbolic acts intended to show a dedication of commitment to each other and are not legally binding in any way. *Fifty Shades of Grey* depicts such a contract as part of the story, but people who are new to BDSM or just want experiment have no need for such things.

Bondage

One very popular and common aspect of BDSM games is Bondage, which is the act of restraining another person. Many couples enjoy using bondage during sex, even if they don't think of themselves as belonging to that subculture. The act of restraining one's partner (as long as they consent) can be extremely erotic and sensual. Bondage can be done in a variety of ways with items that are easy to obtain.

Shackles and Handcuffs

Shackles and Handcuffs can be purchased at sex shops and novelty stores. Use them to bind the Sub's wrists or ankles in a variety of positions. Keep their hands bound behind their back, cuff them spread eagle to the four corners of a bed, bind them bent over at the waist with their wrists attached to their ankles, or much more. As long as you're acting safely, both parties enjoy and consent to it, and you both feel sexual pleasure; the only limit is your imagination. Just remember to pay attention to where you put the key.

Ropes

Ropes are another great tool for bondage and there's no risk of losing the key. Rope can be purchased anywhere, including; hardware stores, sporting goods stores, and even grocery stores. Soft, wide ropes are the most comfortable for the wearer and the easiest to work with. They tangle less, don't damage the skin, and are easiest to untie. Thin ropes can possibly cut the skin, especially if the sub strains against them, and they can be more difficult to untie. Be sure to void rough ropes that can cause painful rashes and abrasions, lessening the fun and leading to possibly embarrassing questions.

Besides ropes, Bondage can be performed with a wide variety of other common household items including; scarves, belts, neckties, duct tape, plastic utility ties, bungi cords, clothing, chains, ribbons, elastic bands, or anything else you can think of. Just remember that safety always comes first. Never bind a person so tightly that their circulation is hindered or their skin is bruised, cut, or damaged. Many professional and experienced Dominants recommend allowing the Submissive to hold their own bindings, so they have the ability to release it and untie themselves whenever they want to. A little practice and some trial and error will help you find the best methods for bondage that work for you and your partner.

Now, for some inspiration, here's a fun short story that may help you and your play partner think of some creative ideas of your own.

Alyssa Plays Sex Slave

Alyssa had both been curious about BDSM for a while, but had never had the guts to try it before now. She talked with her boyfriend Kevin about it and they both decided to try it. Over several dates, they talked about what kind of things they wanted to try together and picked their safe words and. Now it was finally the night for the big date they had both been waiting for. Kevin locked the hotel room door and waited for her to immerge from the bathroom, pacing the room nervously.

Kevin drew in his breathe as Alyssa stepped out wearing the new lingerie she had purchases special for tonight. It was a black lace negligee with matching silk panties. Black thigh-high stockings and a pair of black stilettos made her legs look even longer and a black choker necklace completed the ensemble. He'd never seen her looking so beautiful or so sexy.

"Welcome home, Sir" she said, playing the role of the Submissive. She felt silly and awkward, but she liked it too. It felt naughty, taboo, and sexy to be playing her boyfriends sex slave. She wrapped her arms around his neck and kissed him passionately on the lips.

Kevin gently removed her hands from around his neck and placed them at her sides, holding them there. "Naughty girl." He chastised playfully. He felt awkward too in his new role playing her Dominant, but it was thrilling and made him feel more aroused than ever before. He said to her, "I'm the one in charge tonight. You are not to do anything without my permission, including kissing or touching me. I will train you on how a proper slave behaves. Lay down on the bed."

Alyssa did as she had been told, and lay in the center of the hotels king-sized bed. Kevin said, "Good girl. Now put your hands behind your head and keep them there until I give you permission to move them. I want you to lie perfectly still while I have my way with you."

"Yes, Sir." Alyssa smiled. It was strangely thrilling to be commanded in this way and she felt her body tingling with sexual excitement. She forced herself not to move as Kevin slowly kissed all over her body. He started with her feet, removing her heels, and massaging her toes. He kissed his way up her calves, to the curve of her thighs, where he stripped her of her stockings one by one.

Alyssa gasped with pleasure as Kevin kissed along the outside her silk panties, then slowly removed them, sliding them sensually off her hips. She thought he would kiss her bare sex then, but he cruelly made her wait, drawing out the anticipation in a way that drove her wild.

Her black lace negligee had a silk ribbon that laced all the way up the front. As he slowly untied it, he kissed the delicate flesh as it was exposed, until the nightie was completely opened and her luscious breasts were set free. As Kevin kissed and suckled her sensitive nipples, Alyssa moaned and arched her back, pushing herself towards him. Although he had touched her breasts many times before, it had never felt as amazing as it did tonight within the setting of their game. Not being able to touch him and giving over her power to him, heightened the sexual pleasure for both of them and lifted them to a new level of arousal.

"Naughty girl." Kevin admonished as she squirmed with delight. "I told you to lay still. If you can't obey, I will just have to tie you down."

Alyssa bit her lip and strained to keep her body motionless as Kevin pleasured every inch of her body with his hands, lips, fingers and mouth. He suckled her nipples, kissed her stomach and thighs, and squeezed her buttocks. Knowing she couldn't move made her want to run her hands over his muscular body. The agony of not being permitted to was just so damn hot; she couldn't believe how turned on she was. Kevin knew he was driving her crazy, and it made him all the harder for her too.

Finally, his mouth worked its way to the delicate triangle of her most intimate folds. His voice was a husky growl as he said "Spread your thighs and hold them open wide with your hands."

Alyssa obeyed, and Kevin rewarded his little sex slave by making love to her with his mouth. He suckled and lapped with his tongue in just the right spot while she panted and gasped with pleasure. Soon, he knew she was about to orgasm. Thrusting his fingers inside of her, he commanded forcefully, "Climax for me, slave! I want to hear it!"

Alyssa let herself go, crying out loudly as the power of her orgasm rocketed through her body. Kevin stared mesmerized by the beauty of her as she came beneath the touch of his hand and felt exhilarated that he had the power to make her feel that way.

When at last the waves of her climax had ebbed, Kevin climbed onto the bed and lay naked beside her. "Now it's your turn to pleasure me, slave. I want you to use only your mouth and no other part of your body, including your hands."

"Yes, Sir." Alyssa smiled; eager to obey his command. She delighted in pleasuring him as he had done for her. She started with his neck, kissing her way down his strong shoulders. She made a trail of delicate kisses along his arms, hands, and suckled on his fingers. She licked playfully at his nipples, biting them playfully with her teeth. Finally, she kissed her way down his stomach, to find the most sensitive part of him erect and ready. She made love to him with her mouth while wrapped his hands through her hair and groaned with intense pleasure. Alyssa's tongue danced playfully along the length of him, before taking him fully into her mouth and devouring him hungrily.

"I want you to get on top of me." Kevin commanded and she mounted herself on top of him. They both moaned with pleasure as he thrust deep inside her hot, wet body.

Bracing her hands against his chest, Alyssa began to stroke up and down the length of him with her hips, but Kevin grabbed her hands and pulled them to her sides, holding her captive in his grip.

"Naughty girl. What do I keep telling you?" Kevin glared playfully; enjoying the role he had taken on and sending thrills of excitement through Alyssa. "I am in charge and you need my permission to touch me."

"Sorry, Sir" Alyssa said, her entire body was going crazy with desire. She'd never wanted to touch him so badly in her entire life.

"Now, put your hands on your thighs and don't touch me again." Kevin commanded. Alyssa grasped her own thighs and used them for leverage as she continued to thrust slowly on top of him. Kevin grasped her firmly by the waist to help balance, protecting her from falling.

He said to her, "Good girl, now I want you to pull up to the very end of me, then slide all the way back down again, as deep as you can, as slowly as you can."

Alyssa moaned and panted as she moved slowly up and down over the full length of Kevin's throbbing manhood. She was soaking wet with the fluids of her own juices and he could feel her muscles rippling around him. He commanded her to move faster and harder, and he could sense the climax building within them both. Then he told her to let loose with abandon. She pumped as hard and fast as she could, throwing back her head, while he drove his hips up to meet her thrusts, until suddenly they both climaxed together, moaning and crying out in unison. It was the best sex either of them had ever had and they knew without a doubt that they would play this game again.

How to Role Play

The character Christian Grey has created his own playroom dungeon where he can act out his fantasies in BDSM role playing games with his partner, but you don't need to remodel your house or buy a lot of expensive equipment to have a good time.

All you need is a little imagination and the rest is as easy as one, two, three.

Picking a Fantasy Role to Play

Number One: decide which role you would like to play in your fantasy sex game. Just think about what fantasies turn you or who you've always wanted to be. Would you like to play doctor and patient, or perhaps doctor and nurse? Maybe you'd like to be Tarzan and Jane or a Knight and Princess. Perhaps one of you always wanted to be a police officer, secretary, castaway, school teacher, pirate, or anyone else you can imagine. Remember, the fun of becoming someone else is that you're free to enjoy sex without the burdens of regular life intruding in, so don't be afraid to be creative, wild, silly, or even naughty.

Setting the Scene

Number Two: after you and your partner have decided what roles you both want to play, try to create as detailed a scene as you can. Some fantasies don't require much work at all, like pretending to be a prostitute with a client, where all you really need is a skimpy dress and some imagination. Other fantasies can get as elaborate as you want to make them, like pretending to be a king having an affair with maiden. Setting the scene where your fantasy will take place adds life and atmosphere to your game and can heighten the fun of your experience. Best of all, it doesn't have to be complex, expensive, or time consuming.

Location

One easy way to set the scene for your fantasy is to go someplace new. Whether it's a private office, a cheap motel, an extravagant hotel, or a secluded beach; getting away from your regular bedroom and going someplace out of the ordinary helps create the illusion that you're in a different world. If going away isn't an option, just changing things at home can make a big difference. Move the furniture around, go to a room you don't seldom use, or try something as simple as changing the comforter on your bed.

Lighting

Another way to set the scene is with lighting. The soft glow of candles, the direct light of a interrogation lamp, the pitch blackness of a blindfold, or the pulsing of a disco strobe light are all great ways to immerse yourself into your fantasy. Don't forget the way colored light bulbs can affect the mood of a room too. Everything your eyes can or cannot see will help add to your fun.

Music

You can also set the scene in a room by playing different types of music. The right music selection can create almost any mood, and even evoke feelings of different locations or periods in time. There are jazz band recordings, Celtic chants, heavy metal rock music, sounds of the rain forest, romantic love songs, and everything in between. Whatever atmosphere you're looking to create, someone has made a soundtrack for it.

Costumes

One of the easiest ways to enhance your fantasy is with costumes. Lingerie shops often have outfits specifically designed for erotic role playing, including French maid and nurses uniforms, masquerade masks, and more. You can also shop at regular costume stores or clothing shops for fun things to wear, such as lingerie, boots, hats, gloves, stockings, scarves, belts, and more. Sometimes the items you need for role playing can even be found in your own closet or garage.

For inexpensive costume ideas, try shopping at Thrift stores. Many people donate their old uniforms, vintage outfits, and even brand new clothing that has never been worn. You can sometimes find prom dresses, fire fighter helmets, athletic uniforms, biker jackets, or whatever else turns you on. One of the benefits about buying costumes from thrift shops is that they're cheap enough you won't mind cutting them up. With just a few snips with a pair of scissors, any outfit can be given playful peak holes, a shorter hemline, or torn to show more bare flesh.

Collars

Collars can be purchased at adult entertainment shops, lingerie stores, grocery stores, or even pet stores. The Submissive wears the collar around their throat as a sensual symbol of their subservience. Make certain that anything worn around the throat is loose enough for unrestricted breathing and does not chafe the skin. Collars can be used in lots of fun ways, including walking the Submissive with a leash or tying them to a headboard. Many people like to where them strictly as ornamentation and find them visually stimulating.

Props

In addition to costumes, props can provide a new level of detail and realism to your fantasy, allowing you to really enjoy your role. If you're playing a prison warden, it's expected that you'll have a uniform and handcuffs, but you can enhance the role even more with a plastic toy gun and baton from a toy store. When it's time to book your prisoner try dipping their fingertips in chocolate to perform a mock fingerprinting session and then licking it off   Finally, refer to bars on your headboard as a jail cell before performing a very erotic strip search of the prisoner. The more details in your fantasy the more you can both surrender to the pleasures you find and the more fun you'll have.

If you like playing doctor or nurse, stop at medical supply store from some fun props, just remember safety always comes first and be certain to remove anything sharp or dangerous before you play. If he like French maids purchase a real feather duster and let her clean every inch of his naked body.   If she likes cowboys, find a straw hat, some leather chaps and discover a new use for a lasso.

Props can be found absolutely everywhere. Adult shops are a good place to buy sex toys, but don't limit your imagination only to traditional gimmicks. Remember that every-day household items can be used in new and creative ways. Clothes pins aren't just for hanging laundry; they can also make great nipple clamps. That old scarf in your dresser can be a blindfold. The kitchen is a true treasure chest of toys, with all its wooden spoons, plastic spatulas, ice-cube trays, and cans of whipped cream. With just a little imagination, your home is toy store ready for experimentation and adventure.

Trying New Things

Number Three: trying new things is the best part of fantasy role playing. By pretending to someone else, we lower our inhibitions and become willing to do things we never would have dared to do before. The atmosphere you create is just a way to immerse yourself into the role playing fantasy, but the ultimate purpose of the game is to enhance your sexual pleasure by trying new things.

At first, the simply the act of role playing is new enough to create sexual excitement all by itself. As you get more comfortable with the game however, you'll be able to try increasingly more new things within the realm of the fantasy. Just remember to always keep safety your top priority, and that your partner consents to everything and finds pleasure in it. If you play games that involve any sort of bondage, punishment, or pain, make sure that every safety precaution is used, including safe words and safe gesture. By keeping safe, you can keep the game pleasurable, consensual, and fun; so let your imagination run wild.

If your partner agrees, you might enjoy trying some new positions and fetishes. Books and movies can provide plenty of creative ideas, and so can your own imaginations. You might like to try tickling, sensory deprivation, spanking, or others. You may want to explore different methods of sex, like oral techniques, sodomy, or perhaps even tantric sex.

As you get more comfortable exploring, you may both like to try different variations of your role playing fantasy, like changing roles. If she has been playing the prisoner and he's been playing the pirate, it might be a lot of fun to switch roles and let her have her way with him instead. It might be fun to try playing completely different roles or games all together. If a particular fantasy isn't as fun as you had hoped it would be, just stop playing it and go back to what you like. Sexual fantasy and role playing is all about pleasure, so when you find what you like it's good to keep doing it, but that doesn't mean you can't try something completely new every now and then too.

Here is another fun short story to give you some ideas of just how far imagination can take you.

Playing Knight of the Princess

Charles had rented the secluded mountain cabin for the entire weekend. Surrounded by a pine forest, it was the perfect place to escape their busy careers and enjoy each other.

"This place is beautiful!" Beth said with bright eyes, as he gave her a tour of the inside. There was a stone fireplace in the center, surrounded by plush furniture and even a large hand-woven rug. The Kitchen was fully equipped with a dining table romantically set for two. A vase full of local wildflowers sat in the center of the table, and a bottle of wine chilled in a bucket of ice nearby. The bedroom had magnificent four poster bed made out of carved oak. The cabin was the perfect setting for the romantic weekend they had planned.

"I'll cook us dinner while you get changed." Charles said. "As soon as you're ready, we can begin playing."

"Start playing as soon as I come out of the bedroom!" Beth beamed, already aroused with excitement. She'd been looking forward to this moment all week, and now that it was here she couldn't wait to get started.

She carried her bag of play clothes into the bedroom while Charles started cooking in the kitchen. She pulled on black thigh-high stockings and attached them to the garter straps of her full bodice corset. On top of the undergarments, she put on a long dress she'd found in a thrift shop and reminded her of a princess of yore. It was made of a white silky material trimmed with gold and buttoned all the way down the front. She knew the outline of the black undergarments would be visible through the sheer white fabric and guessed correctly that it would drive Charles wild with desire. Next she adorned herself with play jewelry, put on her highest heels, and strode nobly from the bedroom like a princess should.

Charles's eyes glimmered with lust just looking at her and he felt himself become erect. Eager to begin their game, he knelt on one knee, and bowed low before her. "My Lady, you look lovely as the night sky this evening."

Beth peered down at him regally and said. "I am chilled. Build me fire, knight to ward off the cold."

"As you wish, my Lady." Charles said with a humble bow. Beth enjoyed watching his muscles flex as he carried the heavy logs and set to work building a fire for her in the stone fireplace. Soon the cabin was glowing with bright flames.

"I fear I have made the fire too large, my Lady" Charles said with a mischievous grin.

"Foolish knight; now I am getting hot. Remove my clothing so I can cool down." Beth insisted.

"As you command, my Lady." Charles knelt before her and slowly unfastened the buttons of her white dress from the bottom up. When her sexy leg protruded from the open garment, he couldn't resist kissing her flesh tenderly. The next button to be undone revealed her thigh, and he kissed her there too. The sensuous touch of his lips sent thrills of pleasure shooting through her body and she sighed softly.

Slowly, Charles worked his way up, kissing her body as it was slowly revealed with each button he unfastened. Beth's skin tingled with anticipation as he came to her panties and kissed her sex through the thin fabric.   Charles continued to work his way up her body, kissing her stomach through her corset, until he came to the luscious mounds of her cleavage.   Beth closed her eyes and ran her fingers through his hair as he kissed her swelling breasts as much as they were exposed before continuing on.

He kissed his way up her shoulders, to the hollow of her throat, up her neck, and ended with a deeply passionate kiss on her lips.   He ran his fingers through her hair, and Beth opened her mouth to him. Their tongues intertwined, until finally they pulled apart from their embrace, gasping for air. He stepped away from her then, and removed her dress off her shoulders and folded it neatly.

"How may I please you next, my Lady?" he asked, panting with desire.

"I'm still too warm. Undress me the rest of way." Beth said, panting with lust. She had never wanted anyone more than she wanted him at this moment.

Eager to obey, Charles walked around behind her, and began to untie the intricate laces that bound her corset closed. He kissed her neck and the back of her shoulders, as bit by bit he opened the laces of her corset. Once the garment was completely opened, he pulled it away her from her body, setting her ample breasts free. Her nipples puckered at the sudden exposure to the air, and she brought her hand to them, fondling herself sensually. Still standing behind her, Charles massaged her back and shoulders with firm movements of his hands, pressing his fingers into her muscles in just the right way. She sighed contentedly, enjoying in the pampering.

Next, he came around front and knelt in front of her at her feet. He carefully removed her high heels, kissing her feet playfully as he did so. Then he kissed her inner thigh, until he came to the place where her stockings were held in place by her garter straps. He unhooked the garters, and pulled her sticky wet panties down off her hips, as she stepped out of them. She parted her thighs invitingly and Charles kissed gently along her labia, all the way to her clitoris, making love to her with mouth while she curled her fingers through his hair and moaned. Before long, she was climaxing as his tongue worked furiously to please her and her cries of ecstasy filled the cabin.

"How may I serve you now, my Lady?" he asked as her moans slowly ebbed. She ordered him to strip off his clothes and lay naked on the giant run on the floor. Eagerly, Charles did as he'd been told. His giant erection, pointing straight towards the ceiling.

Beth strode to the cabins kitchen and returned with a bowl of ice. Straddling him with the soaking wet folds of her sex just inches from his erection, she said playfully "There is a traitor amongst the knights of my army. Is it you?"

"No, I would never betray you my Lady."
Charles said. Suddenly, he felt the freezing burn of
ice as she applied it to the sensitive flesh of his organ
and caressed him with it.

"Tell me the truth and I'll save you from this
torture." She taunted playfully, just as they had
agreed on when they discussed their play-time ideas.

Charles writhed and moaned with delighted
pleasure as Beth caressed his organ with the ice and
then enveloped him with the hot wet folds of her sex.
The "torture" lasted until she felt him nearing orgasm.
Then they moved the game to the kitchen and had
wild intercourse bent over the dining room table as
they both climaxed together in perfect unison. When
they were both finally satisfied and cuddled in bed,
exhausted and happy, they agreed that while this
weekend had been great, next weekend they would
try a new scenario; perhaps cops and robbers.

"You did a great job being the Dominant this
time." Charles said, "But I think I'd like another turn at
it."

"Sure!" Beth agreed; liking to play either role.
"How about next time you play the brash rogue pirate
and I play the innocent virgin?"

Charles grinned; already thinking of ideas.

Sensory Deprivation

In the book and movie *Fifty Shades of Grey*, Christian heightens Anastasia's senses through sensory deprivation in order to increase her feelings of pleasure. As long as it is consensual you and your partner can try this same technique to maximize your feelings of pleasure too.

It has long been proven that depriving a human being of one of their senses can heighten their perception of their remaining ones and make them more sensitive. Members of the BDSM community have used this fact to heighten their partner's sexual pleasure. They want to heighten the sense of touch, and found it fun and effective to do so by depriving play partners of senses like sight or sound. In return, their play partner often experiences a greater awareness of every sensation that pulses through their bodies, including sexual pleasure and orgasm.

Blindfolds

Sight is a very popular sense that many people like to be deprived of during sex. It is a common practice to turn off the lights when couples make love in the blackness of night. However, you can submerge your play partner into darkness any time by blindfolding them while you can see their body easily in the light and know exactly where and how to touch them.

When your play partner is blindfolded, they will not be able see you at all, or know where, when, or how you are going to touch them next. It adds an exhilarating element of excitement and anticipation when every touch is a surprise, and they are left wondering what will happen next. With the senses heightened in this way, every touch becomes exponentially more erotic for both of you.

In *Fifty Shades*, Christian places ear phones into Anastasia's ears, making her only able to hear music and nothing depriving her of her sense of hearing. This could easily be accomplished at home with headphones, ear plugs, and/or music.

Some people like to enhance their play partner's pleasure with their sense of smell. Try places scented candles or fresh flowers in the room, spraying perfumes, or using anything else that creates an erotic scent. Run a flower across your blindfolded partners face, hold a ripe strawberry beneath their nose and against their lips, or their favorite red wine.

Here is another short story to inspire you and play partner and show you just how fun it can be to be senseless.

Senseless Pleasures

Julie opened her eyes to complete and utter darkness. Not even a glimmer of light shone through the thick blindfold that covered her eyes and submerged into blackness. It was a strange feeling not being able to see anything, and more erotic than she would have thought.

She was completely naked, lying on a large bed, atop silky sheets. She was keenly aware the soft feel of the fabric where it touched her bare flesh and could feel her skin prickling with goose bumps where the gentle breeze of the ceiling fan grazed her. The sensation made her nipples grow taut and she raised her hands to caress them, liking the way it heightened her arousal.

Suddenly, she heard footsteps into the room and smiled, knowing it was her play partner, Jeff. He caressed her cheek with something soft, and she startled at the unexpected touch. It took her only a moment to warm to the sensation, as he repeated the motion, gently brushing her cheek with something velvety soft and wonderfully fragrant.

"A rose?" she guessed.

"Yes." Jeff confirmed. He caressed the flower under her jaw line, down her long neck to the hollow of her throat. Julie arched her back and sighed with pleasure as the soft rosebud moved over her breasts, circling her nipples as he kissed them with his hot mouth, and nipped at them with his teeth. When the flower trailed down the muscles of her stomach, across her inner thigh, to the folds of her sex, she gasped aloud with pleasure as he suddenly brought his lips to her most sensitive fold.

Julie spread her thighs wide, giving him better access, and moaned aloud as Jeff licked the folds of her labia and found his way to clitoris, where he licked and suckled until she was writhing on the bed, delirious with pleasure.

"I want you inside me!" she gasped, arching her hips and running her long fingernails through this hair, begging him to enter her. Suddenly, she felt the sensation of Jeff's finger slowly entering her. He added a second finger and then a third and she bucked her hips, meeting him thrust for thrust.

"Come for baby. I want to watch you orgasm while I touch you." Jeff said in a voice thick with lust.

He used the fingers of his left hand to massage her clitoris in just the right way, while he continued to make love to her with the fingers of his left. The stimulation was more than Julie could stand and she orgasmed loudly, screaming out in pleasure as he watched. When as last the waves of her climax had subsided she felt a new sensation caressing her cheek and knew right away that it was his erect manhood and opened her mouth to him.

"If you can find this, you can have it." Jeff teased and pulled slightly away from her, but still within her reach.

Still blindfolded, Julie groped in the dark, finding erection and using her fingers, hands, lips, mouth and tongue to make love to him. She could hear his groans of pleasure, but better than that she could feel the flexes and twinges of his organ as she sucked, licked, and fondled him. She had never paid attention to such things before and was amazed how much information she could gather that way on knowing just how to touch him.

"Careful, you're getting me too hot!" Jeff groaned and removed himself from her mouth.

Julie searched in the dark for him, but all she found was empty mattress. Was he still there, watching her? Had he left her alone? Julie didn't want to fall off the bed, so she soon gave up and contented herself to lie on the silky sheets, gently touching herself. It felt good and she slowly increased her masturbation, until her breathing began to quicken.

Suddenly she felt a freezing cold pain upon both her nipples and cried out in surprise.

"Don't stop, keep going." She recognized Jeff's voice. "This is just a little something to help you stay cool."

Julie gasped again as the freezing cold pain was applied to her nipples again and came to realization that Jeff was holding ice cubes to them. She squirmed in an effort to get away from the burning cold, but it was useless. She couldn't see where Jeff was, but he could see her easily. The freezing pain was oddly pleasurable and definitely erotic. As she continued to masturbate, she found that she was far more wet and easily stimulated than she had been just moments before.

She felt Jeff climb onto the bed and lay beside her. He put her hands on his body so she could tell exactly where he was. He stroked his rock hard organ with one hand and caressed the muscles of his chest with the other while he took over the task of massaging her dripping wet folds with the fingers of one hand while flicking her freezing cold nipples with the other. The feeling made thrills of pleasure rocket through her body and made her go wild with desire.

"I want you!" she moaned, and waited in eager anticipation for what incredible pleasure was going to come next.

Prolonging the Fun

In the book *Fifty Shades of Grey*, every time Christian Grey has a sexual encounter with Anastasia, he makes it a priority to give her sexual pleasure before satisfying himself. He is the Dominant or Master in their relationship and Anastasia is his Submissive or Sex Slave, so one might have the false assumption that their game would be all about him commanding her to pleasure him, but they are actually the complete opposite. One of the reasons *Fifty Shades of Grey* gained such huge popularity was because it was all about how Anastasia received orgasm after orgasm from Christian, before he ever thought about having one himself. Readers found this to be romantic, appealing, and sexy as hell. Make sure to include plenty of foreplay in your role playing games and you will be too.

Once a man has an orgasm, the act of sex is pretty well finished for at least for several hours. It's not bias, it's simple biology. So why do so many lovers make male orgasm their goal? It's ridiculous to rush to be finished with sex when it feels so incredibly good to be having it. So make prolonging sex instead of ending it your goal and you'll be surprised at how long you can make the fun last.

Christian Grey made it his goal to give Anastasia Steele multiple orgasms almost every time they had sex. Only when she was satisfied did he allow himself to enter her body and have an orgasm himself. For a man to give a woman multiple orgasms takes patience, but he will find the results are well worth the effort and will not be feeling left in by the end. The key to great orgasms is foreplay, and lots of it.

Foreplay

For incredible results, it is important to make foreplay about the entire body. Our skin, which covers our bodies from head to toe, is full of tiny nerve endings that are stimulated by the slightest touch. Take advantage of that fact, and find pleasure in every inch of your play partners beautiful flesh.

Upper Body

It's nice to stroke someone's hair, caress their cheek, or kiss their lips; but that doesn't mean you should ignore the rest of their body. Try rubbing your hand along the nape of their neck, nibbling the earlobes, or kissing the delicate hallow of their throat.

The bare shoulder is graceful and elegant. Massage them with slow sensuality. Kiss your way down your partner's body. Guide your hands, fingertips, lips and tongue to all the parts of their naked torso; the back, the, stomach, and the sides of their chest just where the ribs start to curve.   Many people concentrate of just one particular part of the chest, but don't forget the rest of the upper body and your partner will thank you for it.

Find out what drives your play partner wild with passion and give it to them with deliberate sensuality. Their body language, breathing, and subtle movements will let you know when you're doing things right. Let your partner be your guide in how to give them the most sexual pleasure.

Don't make the mistake of doing one thing for too long or repeating the same movements too often. There are many parts of the body to enjoy and explore, and foreplay should be about finding them all.

Lower Body

Pleasure your partner by pampering them from the fee up. Some people like to have their toes sucked or their arches massaged, while others are ticklish. Once again, let their responses be your guide and find out how they like to be pleasured.

Move your way up your partner's calves, slowly working your way to the thighs, hips, and curves of the buttocks. Massage, fondle, kiss, lick, and rub every inch of them before coming to the crowning jewel of their genitals. When you find the places they likes to be touched the most, spend some extra time there. If you accidentally do something they don't like, move on to what they do enjoy. With enough practice and dedication, you should be able to pleasure your partner to into near orgasm with just your fingers, hands, and mouth alone. Save actual intercourse for the very end, like dessert after an amazingly satisfying meal. Sex isn't fast food; it's a six course meal to be savored.

Masturbation

Many sex therapists and couples counselors recommend that partners masturbate together to increase intimacy. Many professionals who work in the adult entertainment industry recommend the practice of self-pleasure as well.

There is no better way to learn what turns you on and brings you to orgasm better than masturbation. Many women use their hands, fingers, sex toys, and vibrators to reach orgasm in private. Many men do the same. Encourage your partner to masturbate along with you when you are being intimate together. Not only is it extremely erotic for partners to view each other masturbating, but it is an excellent way to learn how your partner likes to be touched best to achieve orgasm.

Go ahead and try it with your partner tonight. See how long you can draw foreplay out before you finally succumb to intercourse. I'm sure you will find it a titillating, exhilarating, and rewarding game to play. Here's a short story to help get you in the mood.

Maximum Pleasure

Trevor and Samantha had been nervous about trying BDSM games at first, but they quickly discovered it was their favorite way to have sex. The best part of them was the way it allowed them to draw out the pleasure they each gave each another.

Samantha lay naked on her stomach across their large bed and smiled in happy anticipation. Trevor picked up a bottle of oil from their night stand and began to sensually massage her, paying special attention to her neck, shoulders and lower back. As he eased away all her tensions, Samantha sighed contentedly.

"Roll over so I can massage your front." Trevor commanded and Samantha willingly complied. She shivered excitedly, hoping he would touch her where she liked it most, but he wanted to take his time and draw out her anticipation as long as possible.

He started with her hand, kissing and massaging it. Then he worked his way up her arm to her shoulders, and across to the hollow of her throat, caressing every inch of her with his lips and hands. Samantha leaned back her head and a soft moan escaped her lips, as he kissed up her neck and then back down again to her magnificent breasts.

With slow deliberateness of purpose, Trevor kissed sensuous circles around her breasts before finally taking her right nipple into his mouth. He suckled it while his hand softly squeezed her other nipple between his finger and thumb and gently pinched and pulled it.

Samantha moaned and arched her back, pushing herself towards him, as she ran her hands through his hair, wanting more of him. Trevor alternated back and forth between her left and right nipples, pinching one and suckling the other, then switching again. The louder she moaned, the harder he sucked, loving the powerful feeling he gained from controlling her pleasure and knowing that he could make her come.

Next, Trevor kissed his way down Samantha's flat stomach to the delicate triangle of her sex.

"Spread your thighs." He commanded and she eagerly obeyed. He made love to her then with his mouth; expertly using his tongue and fingers till she was writhing on the bed in ecstasy. Samantha cried out loudly as she climaxed against his touch and he relished the taste of her.

"Very good." Trevor complimented, when at last she had regained her composure.

She looked at him with pleading eyes and he knew she wanted to ask him something.

"You may speak." He permitted.

Smiling gratefully, Samantha said "Please, Sir, may I pleasure you as you've done to me?"

"Yes, but only with your mouth. Put your hands above your head and grip the headboard of the bed." Trevor commanded. Samantha did as she'd been told and Trevor used a short length of rope to bind her slender wrists to the headboard. Then he knelt by her face so she could access his organ and told her she could begin.

Hungrily, Samantha took him into her hot, wet mouth; eager to pleasure him just as he had done for her. He groaned with ecstasy as she licked along the length of him then took the tip fully into her mouth and sucked hard as if she intended to devour him. As she pleasured him with her mouth, he reached down with his fingers as stimulated her already wet folds. She was already so hot, it didn't take long for her to near climax again.

"I bet I can make you orgasm first." Trevor taunted. Samantha sucked his erection even more feverishly in attempt to win the bet, but Trevor extracted himself from her mouth before it was too late.

"That's cheating!" Samantha laughed as she strained against her bonds.

"I don't care. I'm still going to win." Trevor teased and made love to her with his mouth again until she was gasping and moaning with her second orgasm.

Just as it was coming to an end, Trevor slowly inserted his organ into her quivering slot, making her cry out with renewed pleasure. Straining against her bonds, she bucked wildly trying to drive him more deeply into her, but Trevor moved with excruciating slowness, drawing out the act of their love making as long as possible. She felt so tight, so wet, and so incredibly good it took all of his will power not to lose control and buck wildly against her, but seeing how much pleasure he was giving her by drawing things out made it all worth it and increased his pleasure more than he ever would have dreamed.

"Harder! Faster! Please!" Samantha begged until finally Trevor could resist no more and let lose his passions, thrusting powerfully into her with wild abandon. Within moments they both climaxed together in a super orgasm that seemed to last and last and last, as wave upon wave of delirious rapture exploded through their bodies. When it finally ebbed, they were both sweating and out of breath, but extremely satisfied.

Sadism and Masochism

As their sexual relationship advances Christian Grey introduces Anastasia to the world of Sadism and Masochism. These games are particularly dangerous and need to be played extreme care. Although they are *Not* for every couple, the ones who love it, really love it!

Sadism is when someone enjoys giving another person physical pain. Masochism is when someone enjoys receiving physical pain. Although Domination and Submissive games can easily be played without including Sadism and Masochism, it is not uncommon for these two types of games to be played together.

Many Dominants are Sadists and like to give punishments to their Submissives if they fail to obey their commands. If the Sub is a Masochist, the act of receiving a punishment of physical pain, like a spanking, is more pleasure than actual punishment and they really enjoy the experience.

The nerve pathways that transmit physical pleasure, such as those felt during orgasm, are the same nerve pathways that transmit pain. So, the line between sexual pleasure and physical pain is very thin and easily crossed. For Masochists, there is no difference between the two and pain can feel as pleasurable as sex.

Taking on the role of a Sadist in sexual play requires a great deal of responsibility. Even though the Masochist may enjoy receiving certain types of pain, it is up to the Sadist to ensure that the pain is delivered in a safe way and doesn't cause permanent injury, become too intense to be enjoyable, or endanger the Masochist's health or life.

Safe Words and Safe Gestures

It is extremely important that all play partners who want to engage in Sadism and Masochism games use safe words and safe gestures. These need to be agreed upon before play begins and checked on during play to confirm they have not been forgotten.

Many couples like to use the safe words Yellow and Red. Yellow means that play is becoming too intense and the Sadist needs to back off a little, and Red indicates that play needs to be stopped immediately. Some couples like to use safe words that are unique, like Madagascar or Hippopotamus. Make sure to choose a word that is unlikely to come up during regular play or normal conversation, or else playtime could be interrupted accidentally.

Sometimes safe words can't be used, such as when the Sub is gagged or short of breath. In these instances, it's important to use safe gestures. A common one is for the Sub to hold an object in their hand, like a scarf. When they want to signal the Dom to stop they simply drop the object, and the game play is immediately ended.

Spanking

The most popular form of Sadism and Masochism is spanking. Many couples engage in a few light spanks during sex without ever realizing they are engaging in BDSM and both partners find it very pleasurable. Spanking can be as light or intense as both partners agree they enjoy. A spanking can range from a single light swat on the butt cheek, to a long procession of full force blows that leave the victim bruised and sore. Most people just use their hand during spanking, but implements can also be used. Examples include paddles, wooden spoons, hair brushes, or anything else with a flat surface.

If both partners want something much more intense than a mere spanking, they can go to the extreme level of using belts, rods, canes, or riding crops. These items are extremely dangerous and can result in serious injury. They should never be used by anyone who hasn't received proper safety training. The use of safety words and the clear consent of their partner are an absolute must.

Hot Wax

Some people enjoy having hot wax drizzled onto their naked bodies. The sensation can range from a comfortable warm feeling to a stinging burn, depending on how hot and intense both partners enjoy. I suggest using unscented candles. They create wax that has a cooler temperature, while the oils in perfumed candles often cause them to burn hotter and they can potentially burn the skin.

Before you begin hot wax play, rub oil on the victim's skin so the wax won't stick directly to their flesh. Once the candle has melted into liquid wax, hold it above the victim and very carefully drizzle small amounts of wax on various parts of their body. For cooler wax, holds the candle higher above the victim so the wax has more time to cool before it reaches their skin. Holding the candle closer to their body will give the wax less time to cool, if they like it hotter on their skin.   For beginners, start with small amounts of wax and drizzle it from a greater height until they build up a tolerance, then slowly lower the distance as they become accustomed to the feeling. Create fun patterns and designs if you like; then have fun peeling the hardened wax away.

Whips and Floggers

Some couples enjoy games that involve whipping. There are many different types of whips, some more painful and dangerous than others. Whips with a mass of short, flat, suede tails are called a flogger. Although they look vicious, they are actually one of the most gentle of whips. The broad surface area of the tails, and the large heavy amount of them, creates a lot of wind resistance, so the tails of a flogger move quite slowly with a minimal impact against the victim's skin.

A flogger can be used to tickle the flesh by moving it across the skin like a feather duster for fun results. They can also be used to lightly smack against the skin to awaken the nerves and heighten the senses. More advanced players can use a flogger with more intensity, however proper safety and training must be retained first so as not to inflict any true harm. Fans of whipping often say floggers are their favourite.

Whips that are longer and thinner inflict a lot more pain than floggers, since they can cut through the air at a much faster rate, building up more speed and applying more force against the body. When more force is applied to a smaller area of flesh, the pain and risk of physical injury increase vastly.

Long whips also pose additional danger because they can wrap around the victim's body and inflict damage to unintended places and organs. If an untrained Sadist is intending to strike their Sub on the back, and their whip accidentally wraps around the torso and strikes their victim in the liver or kidneys, they can cause permanent internal injuries. If you are interested in whipping make sure you get the proper training before you ever attempt the act, even with a willing partner. Stick to the act of spanking in the meantime.

Fun Easy Pains

Of course there is a lot more to Sadism and Masochism games than just whipping and spanking. For those who enjoy it and have a consenting partner, there are lots of fun and easy ways to invoke pain that are less intimidating, but still stimulating and very erotic. One very popular example is rubbing ice cubes against one another's bodies for a freezing pain this is extremely pleasurable.

Another very popular form of Sadism/Masochism is pinching your partner's nipples. Many people find this very enjoyable. If your partner agrees you can try making things more intense by using clips, clamps, or clothes pins.

Here is a stimulating tale to inspire you on how you can role play sadism and masochism with a willing play partner.

Meghan's Spanking

Mike felt excited as he sat behind his desk his office at home and waited for his play partner Meghan. When she finally walked through the door, she looked positively sexy in her "school girl" outfit that she'd managed to put together from things in her closet. She wore a white cotton blouse that clearly revealed the fact that she didn't have on a bra, a short pleated skirt, white knee socks, white cotton panties, and black loafers. To complete the costume, she wore a blue tie and had put her hair in a high ponytail.

"You wanted to see me Professor?" Meghan asked, playing the role of a naughty student.

"Yes, please shut the door." Mike said with a stern look, playing the role of the angry professor. "I called you in here, because we found this in your room. Is it yours?"

He opened his top desk drawer and pulled out a small plastic vibrator and set it on his desk with an accusing glare.

"Maybe" Meghan said, with an insolent tone. She clicked on the vibrator and held it to herself outside her white cotton panties, pleasuring herself with it and panting softly. Her free hand moved up under her blouse, fondling her own breasts. She closed her eyes, moaning, while Mike watched with lust burning in his eyes.

After a few moments he grabbed the vibrator away from her and clicked it off with an angry frown. He grabbed her by the arm said "Masturbating his forbidden on school grounds. Now you must be disciplined for your naughty. Take off your panties and bend over my desk so I can punish you."

His command was sharp and firm and Meghan obeyed, slowly stripping out of her panties sensually. He said, "Quit stalling. Bend over my desk now and lay your cheek flat against it."

"Please don't spank me." Meghan pleaded with big scared eyes. The words were objecting, but they were not her safe words and they both knew it was part of the game. When they planned the role playing scene together, she had told Mike she wanted to beg him not punish her, so he knew she still wanted to play unless she said her safe words.

Mike gripped her firmly by the ponytail and pushed her down forcefully against the desk. "I told you to bend over!"

He forced Meghan down over the desk and positioned her so her hands were gripping the sides and her bare ass was beautifully exposed in the air in a most vulnerable state.

Slowly, he raised the hem of her short pleated skirt and tucked it into the waist band so it was out of the way. Her naked ass was so beautiful with its smooth skin and round cheeks. He knew this spanking excited her as much as it excited him. He could wee that her entire body was quivering with eager anticipation and there was moisture growing between her thighs.

He rubbed her butt cheeks delicately with his hand, caressing her soft skin. Then Mike raised his hand up and brought it crashing against her left butt cheek. She cried out in surprise more than pain, as he spanked her again. Every time his hand struck her bare flesh, it vibrated through both their bodies with delicious power. He spanked her again and again, pausing between each swat to massage her sore and tender buttocks with his hand for a moment before striking her again. Soon his hand was red and stinging almost as much as her bruised ass and he stopped.

"Do you know why I had to discipline you?" Mike asked Meghan in a stern voice.

"Because I disobeyed the rules." Meghan said. Her voice was hoarse with sobs.

"Good girl. Now stand up." She got up from off the desk and rubbed her bruised and swollen butt cheeks, finally letting the tears spill from her eyes.

Mike wiped away her tears and said tenderly, "When you get the need to masturbate, I want you to come to my office and tell me right away. I'll help you to keep from breaking the rules so you don't get in trouble in any more."

"How will you do that, Sir?" Meghan asked. Her eyes were cast downward submissively and she was no longer arrogant or insolent.

"Like this." Mike said, and he made sweet, sensual love to her on top of his desk, pleasuring every inch of her until she orgasmed over and over again.

Summing It All Up

So now you know all the factors you need to know to create your own *Fifty Shades of Grey*. There is no limit to what you and your play partner can do together with a little imagination. Just remember to put safety above all else and keep honest and open communication going with your play partner so that the games you play are equally pleasurable for both of you. Now take what you've learned, talk with partner, and enjoy the fun world of BDSM!

Printed in Great Britain
by Amazon.co.uk, Ltd.,
Marston Gate.